You CAN Write
50,000 Words
in 30 Days

You CAN WRITE

50,000

words in 30 days

DJ MYNATT

S & G
PUBLISHING

YOU CAN WRITE 50,000 WORDS IN 30 DAYS
COPYRIGHT © 2015 BY DJ MYNATT

LIBRARY OF CONGRESS CATALOGING-IN-PUBLICATION DATA
MYNATT, DJ.
    YOU CAN WRITE 50,000 WORDS IN 30 DAYS / DJMYNATT.

ISBN-13: 978-0692470473   (TRADE PAPERBACK)
1. BIOGRAPHY & AUTOBIOGRAPHY / PERSONAL MEMOIRS.
2. RELIGION / CHRISTIAN LIFE / INSPIRATIONAL. 3. HUMOR /
GENERAL.

                                    2015909718

S&G Publishing, Knoxville, TN
www.sgpublish.com

Scripture quotations are from the Holy Bible (KJV)

This content has not been reviewed by The Office of Letters and Light, known as the National Novel Writing Month – or NaNoWriMo – and is not endorsed by them in any way. For more information about the National Novel Writing Month, please visit www.nanowrimo.org

First Printing 2015

Endorsements

"DJ Mynatt went out on a limb to try to write a novel in thirty days and did it! Twice! This easy-to-read memoir is a must for anyone who's heard the "call" to write, but isn't quite sure if she should answer the call...or let it ring."

~ SUZANNE WOODS FISHER
BESTSELLING AUTHOR OF *HEART OF THE AMISH: LIFE LESSONS ON PEACEMAKING AND THE POWER OF FORGIVENESS*

"An engaging, first-hand look at what goes into writing your first novel! DJ Mynatt executes the motions a writer experiences with a tasteful balance of humor and how-to-advice. The perfect guide for all first-time authors."

~ RACHEL MULLER
AUTHOR OF BEST SELLING NOVEL *LETTERS FROM GRACE* & SO YOU THINK YOU CAN WRITE 2012 SEMI-FINALIST.

"A delightful peek into one woman's journey to complete the 50,000 words in a month NaNoWriMo challenge. Mynatt's blog entries are inspirational and she offers an inside view of how she stayed motivated throughout the month and ultimately reached her goal--twice!"

~ RUTH REID
BEST-SELLING AUTHOR OF THE AMISH WONDERS SERIES AND THE HEAVEN ON EARTH SERIES

"If you're thinking about trying NaNoWriMo, get yourself a copy of DJ's book. It's full of practical advice and personal experiences that will help you get the most out of the contest, and maybe even give you the encouragement to finish that book you've always wanted to write!"

~DANA MENTINK
AWARD-WINNING FICTION AUTHOR

"An excellent book for authors and readers alike – not just a "how-to" – this book is a fun and humorous account of how my dear friend wrote her first novel."

~ JC MORROWS
AUTHOR OF SPECULATIVE FICTION AND
PROFESSIONAL BOOK REVIEWER – JCsBookShelf

"*You CAN write 50,000 Words in 30 days*, especially if you read DJ Mynatt's encouraging book that shares her story of entering NaNoWriMo — National Novel Writing Month. DJ Mynatt's instructional guide, daily journaling notes, Bible verses, and follow-up at the end makes a perfect book to transform any wannabe writer into a real author."

~ HOLLY MICHAEL
AUTHOR OF BESTSELLING NOVEL *CROOKED LINES*

Dedication

To Rachel, my amazing daughter – without whom I would never... ever... have considered writing 50,000 words in 30 days!

To Sam and Gwen, my adorable grandchildren – who worked hard to participate alongside their Mom and Grandma. I am immensely proud of them!

To all those who have participated – or plan to participate – in NaNoWriMo, Camp NaNoWriMo, or another writing program...

To my readers, who faithfully read my blog – and continue to encourage me to write!

...and to my Heavenly Father, my Savior, my Comforter, my guide.

Table of Contents

Part 1

INTRODUCTION

CHAPTER 1

The Reason I Write

I have enjoyed reading for as long as I can remember...

I was the youngest of three girls in my family; my sisters were ten and six when I was born. By the time I was old enough to start school, our home had accumulated several bookcases full of books.

My parents bought us mostly **Christian fiction** and **non-fiction** books to read when I was young; we always asked for and received books for birthdays and Christmas... even now I find myself suggesting a book when asked about a gift for myself or a family member. After all, can you ever have enough books?

I read voraciously throughout school, utilizing first the school library, then the local public library, always choosing more and more books to read. Nothing seemed to bring me as much pleasure as opening a book and losing myself in it. And during difficult moments, it became a habit to lose myself in a good book.

I began collecting **Nancy Drew Mysteries** and soon had most, if not all, of them. Through no fault of my own, I lost every one of those books during a difficult time in my marriage, but thankfully, after my two grandchildren were born, I found an opportunity to begin collecting them again. At this moment, I've bought over sixty consecutive books in the series.

Another favorite when I was growing up was **The Bobbsey Twins**; in the past few years, I've been able to find the first dozen books to give as gifts to my grandchildren.

When my aunt gave us some inspirational romances, I was introduced to **Grace Livingston Hill** and **Emily Loring**. In high school, I took a science fiction class and fell in love with **Jules Verne, Carl Sagan, Isaac Asimov, Michael Crichton**, and many others.

When I grew up and married, I continued to read whenever I could find the time. By this time much of what I read, including science fiction and romance novels, were not Christian-oriented. After awhile, I began to notice that I felt depressed after reading some stories – but inspired after reading others.

It would take a great many years for me to make this connection. Noting which books caused these reactions, I soon found a new home for many of them, though it has always been difficult to let go of books – and still is.

While there are some stories that may stir up negative emotions, those that teach us how to overcome problems and make wise choices are worth the effort – and remain on my bookshelves.

Around five years ago, I began reading **Amish fiction**. At the time I believed Amish fiction was a safe choice, with high standards – and for the most part, it was encouraging, as well as entertaining. Unfortunately, I've seen a few that don't quite fit the standards I try to adhere to, so I check out new authors and if there's any doubt, I stay away from them.

The public library is a wonderful place to find new books. Nowadays, once I find a favorite, I buy it in paperback or e-book format (sometimes both if it's one that I enjoy reading a lot). But for years, I have utilized the public library, reserving books online. When I go by to pick them up, I return the ones I have finished; which also gives me a chance to search for new books on the shelves.

———————— nanowrimo ————————

Lots of times I have thought about writing a book of my own, but I expected it to be too difficult... or that I wouldn't have the time... or even more important, that no one would want to read it. But mostly, in a nutshell, I just didn't know how to do it – or how to get started.

Many years ago I actually began a novel... I got a few chapters written, but then work, family, and life got in the way and I never finished it. I put it aside and worked at my full-time job, raising my children and only occasionally thinking of how wonderful it would be if I could find time to write, but honestly never saw myself ever writing again.

Recently several friends have encouraged me to begin writing again. So I searched until I found the old tractor-feed printer pages and re-typed them, using my laptop and word processing software. Now came the hard part... the writing!

The trouble was, what I had written twenty years ago, wasn't necessarily something I would write about today.

———————— nanowrimo ————————

National Novel Writing Month... is where I found my motivation to begin. For the past two years during November, I participated for each of the 30 days of NaNoWriMo – and during November I wrote a blog post for each of the 30 days of NaNoWriMo (granted sometimes it wasn't much, depending on how well my writing was going on the novel).

Not to mention that I had never tried to write a novel, nor had I ever blogged (for you novices out there, that just means I had never written a blog post) until September 2013… when I began not one, but two blogs:

Donna's BookShelf, and

Donna's Family Life

…because, of course, one isn't enough – you have to do more than expected when you're a workaholic!

Donna's BookShelf – my bookshelf blog is used primarily for book reviews. A friend of mine told me I could get free books if I would just write reviews for the publisher (or author). Convinced this was a good idea, I created my daughter created a blog where I could review the free books and I signed up for my first free book. Then a friend said if I was going to blog I could write about my family.

Since my grandchildren live with me, I figured I would have plenty to blog about, so I created a family blog. So far, it's been fun (at least for me). But I don't blog daily... sometimes I go a week or longer. Another blog was begun in April 2014, aptly named:

DJ Mynatt – Inspirational Author

However, this year, after finally realizing that I just couldn't keep up with both, I made the tough choice to combine my family life blog with my new author blog.

In the meantime, I have all sorts of wonderful people who really seem to like my blog posts... and all the time I'm thinking... "What should I write? Am I really reaching anyone?"

Okay, the fact that you're reading this probably should tell me that I am, in fact, reaching others. But what message am I sending out?

———————————————————

But to fully answer the question **"Why Do I Write?"** – I write because I feel I am called, as other Christians are called, to be a witness... to tell others of my belief in God... and that He loves you with an unending love.

I am not such a great witness. I've made many mistakes. I could use the excuse that it's because, although I'm saved by God's grace, I'm still human – and I am drawn to sin as a bee is to honey.

But I have a great desire for others to know of God's love – a love so big, that He gave his only [begotten] son, that whosoever would believe in him should not perish, but have everlasting life (John 3:16).

This is my greatest desire – to be a witness, and a blessing, to others.

For God sent not his Son into the world to condemn the world; but that the world through him might be saved.

~ John 3:17

Chapter 2

How I Got Started

After wishing for much of my life that I would – or could – write a novel, I'm finally taking the plunge! The first step, according to my daughter, was to begin blogging – which would help me to learn to write – if I could just remember to do it.

As I mentioned in the previous chapter, In July 2013, my daughter created a blog and began reviewing books. Soon she was urging me to try it too, and she created a blog just for me. I wrote my very first blog post on August 29, 2013... and I posted my first book review on August 31st.

I posted lots of reviews, mostly of favorite books that I owned. In September, after reading a new book by **Rosemary Hines**, it just made sense to promote the series, as well as the newest book. So I re-read the other two books and posted reviews for all three on my book blog.

The next week I read three books in the **Amish Vines and Orchards** series by **Cindy Woodsmall**. Again I posted a review each day for the books.

The following December, I discovered **Emma Miller**, a wonderful author of Amish novels. At the time, she had seven books about an Amish family. This would be the first time I dedicated an entire week to an author – and a series.

It was so much fun reading – and writing reviews – for the **Hannah's Daughters** series. This was the start of something that was teaching me to write... I just didn't know it at the time. I continued writing reviews for the next six months. Each month I found myself writing more and more reviews.

Then in July 2014, after I received **A Gift of Love** to review, I contacted **Amy Clipston** to ask if I could read and review ALL of her books – maybe feature her for the whole month on my book blog. She was thrilled with the idea and offered to send me any books that I didn't already have.

We worked out a giveaway for the month. My multi-talented daughter put together a banner showcasing all of Amy's books and I began reading and reviewing Amy's books. Wow – it was a lot of work – but I had a lot of fun!

When the month was almost over, I realized I had enjoyed this new idea and I asked Amy if she could recommend a friend or contact another author of Amish Fiction to see if they'd be interested in being my featured author for a month. She recommended **Amanda Flower**, who was interested, but wasn't available until October.

In the meantime I contacted **Vannetta Chapman**. I had read most of her books – and loved them, so I asked if she'd be interested in being featured on my blog. She was happy to be a featured author and after working out the giveaway details, I got started. September was a huge hit!

In October, I featured Amanda – and as I read and reviewed the author's books, I began adding extra details. I was preparing for something big – I just didn't know it at the time. While I was busy featuring Amanda, my daughter had received two new books written by **Laura V. Hilton** to review — **Snow Globe** and **White Christmas in Webster County**.

Once or twice a month, I would take a break from reviewing and just read a novel for fun! So I snatched **Snow Globe** and read it – and LOVED it! I told my daughter and she suggested I feature Laura on my blog. She emailed Laura to see if she was interested... and the rest is history!

For the month of December, I planned to read a few favorite Christmas stories... but once again I made room for another favorite author – **Jennifer Beckstrand** – who is the author of some of my most favorite books! These are the **Huckleberry Hill** series... and these are the books I pick up when I need a hug, or a laugh, or when life gets me down.

January of 2015 I decided to feature debut authors – and I was amazed at the response! I featured a new author every week – for five weeks, and the response from readers was tremendous. Each week I gave away a new book, wrote 1-2 reviews, promoted new books and interviewed the author.

After January was done, I kept going... I have featured authors lined up until September 2015! I was thinking of doing the feature for a year, but since I've had such a great response, I will continue until December 2015... or beyond.

However, I've gotten off track – just a little. So let's go back to the beginning of this adventure... and how I wrote my 50,000 words!

———————— nanowrimo ————————

You might think that working full time, staying busy at home with my family, and featuring an author for an entire month would be enough for anyone...

I certainly thought I was busy. Everything was going fine – until my daughter decided to participate in NaNoWriMo – and decided that good old mom should participate, too.

Every time she gets an idea of something else to get me involved in, my daughter says it's to keep me active physically or to keep my mind busy because Alzheimer's Disease runs in my family.

I appreciate her concern and I try to do my part. But I work a full-time job, fighting traffic all the way there and back. When I get home, there are usually chores to be done and grandchildren that want a little attention. After dinner, it's time to get going on the writing, but by then I'm tired and wanting to go to bed!

When she told me I was going to be writing 50,000 words in 30 days, I honestly didn't think it could be done.

But I did it...

And you can, too!

———————— nanowrimo ————————

What was I thinking???

I'm up at 5:00 AM on weekdays to get ready for work; back home by 5:00 PM most nights. But there's so much to think about – family time, Bible study, errands, meals, getting ready for the next day, as well as looking for time to relax... and my grandchildren need attention, too.

Weekends are even worse! Even if we leave early on Saturday, it's rare to get back home from errands and exercise and whatever else crops up... by mid/ late afternoon.

Now don't get me wrong – I'm not fussing about my life. I enjoy keeping busy... even my relaxing moments are spent knitting while chatting with a friend or while watching a family movie.

It's just that... well, I quickly developed a bad case of cold feet... and they got colder as each day passed... by November 1st they were two blocks of ice!

What I really needed was for the days to fly by... because I really felt that once I had begun, I would begin to enjoy myself... so much that I would be disappointed when December finally arrived

So here's my story of how I wrote over 50,000 words in 30 days... the good, the bad, and the... well, you know.

— nanowrimo —

In the beginning God created the heaven and the earth.

  ~ Genesis 1:1

Chapter 3

National Novel Writing Month

For those who choose to join the "National Novel Writing Month" November challenge – commonly known as NaNoWriMo – and make a commitment to write a novel, bio, or some type of story for 30 days, there are varied results...

1. *those who never sign up*
2. *those who sign up, but never begin*
3. *those who begin, but quit after 1 hour, 1 day, or 1 week*
4. *those who begin and keep writing every day until the 30 days are up, but don't hit the 50,000 mark;*

and...

5. *those who begin and hit the 50,000 mark – or move way past it, as some do... these are the people with the greatest chance of publishing their novels!*

For those of you who read that last line... I am not saying those who hit (or pass) the 50,000 mark are the ONLY ones who have a chance of publishing a novel – just that the ones who take it seriously and write every day, many times passing the daily goal, to get their novel written, are the ones with the greatest chance.

Now... for those who haven't heard of it, or have never participated, here's a little information about how it all began...

National Novel Writing Month, best known as NaNoWriMo, is a writing challenge that puts you in the drivers seat! You choose to participate – the NaNoWriMo challenge is in November of each year, but you can also participate in the Camp NaNoWriMo challenges in April and July of each year.

The very first NaNoWriMo took place in July 1999, in the San Francisco Bay Area. That first year there were twenty-one participants. I'm not sure how they heard of it. Most likely those who were going invited some of their friends, but however it came about, these twenty-one people came together to write for the month of July.

Well, that makes sense... an endeavor such as this would be much easier with support from friends – as well as spending time with others who were trying to accomplish the same task.

Although they may or may not have had any great expectations, none of the participants could have imagined what would occur over the next few years. They merely wanted to band together and write... and they soon discovered that it was actually "fun" – and something they'd like to do again.

The second year took place in November 2000. A friend offered to build a website for the "event" – which had been moved to November so it wouldn't interfere with another event. An email was sent out announcing the start date and sharing the URL of the newly created website. Friends invited friends – who invited more friends.

The twenty-one participants in the first year grew to an unexpected 140 participants in the second year. This was the year Chris discovered that some rules would have to be made... you have to start from scratch, and you can't co-author a book... plus a few others.

Year three, instead of the 150 expected participants, there was an unprecedented 5000 people who wanted to sign up to participate! There were lots of web problems, due mostly to the unexpected traffic, but by Year four, the site was more prepared – for the 14,000 people who signed up!

Year five grew to 25,000 participants.

Year six: 40,000 participants

The now-famous National Novel Writing Month event – ran by the Office of the Letters and Lights group – is an amazing organization! There's lots more history, but you can learn everything you've always wanted to know about NaNoWriMo on its' website. There. Simple.

Just remember, the basic idea of this challenge is simply to sign up by November 1st with a goal to write at least 1,667 words every day – until the 30th.

But the most important fact to keep in mind is that you accept the challenge and participate. Even if you have to quit early or you make it to December but don't reach 50,000 words – you are not a loser. In my opinion, you're still a winner. You did something amazing!

Hey, but don't be telling yourself you can't make it to 50,000 – just keep going, don't give up – and give it all you got. If you do that, whatever your total number of words at the end of 30 days is something to celebrate!

Before I leave this very interesting subject to move on to something dull (just kidding), I want to mention that after just ten years, there were almost 120,000 NaNoWriMo adult participants – with 21,683 winners!

Twenty-one thousand... six hundred... eighty-three people who wrote 50,000 words or more in just 30 days! See... it can be done.

If they can do it...

If I can do it...

YOU can do it.

Trust in the Lord with all thine heart; and lean not unto thine own understanding.

~ Proverbs 3:5

CHAPTER 4

The Challenge

Fifty thousand words…

Thirty days.

Is that even possible?

I don't know what makes it sound easy to some folks – for me, it sounded impossible when I heard it. However, when you have someone who ~~dares~~ challenges you to try it – and you're the sort of person who hates to let others down (or watch family members cross the finish line without you) – you find yourself going "the extra mile".

November 2013 was my first year to sign up for the challenge. I honestly didn't think I could do it – I had always wanted to write a novel, but didn't really know how. I mean, shoot, I could come up with characters, and a fake community, and probably some dialogue, but the story...

How on earth do you make up your own story... especially with a beginning, middle, and end – with interesting events thrown in to gain – and keep – the reader's attention. Come on, what's the point if nobody is going to want to read it? So it has to be interesting... exciting... romantic... daring... even dangerous.

By the way – everyone I talk to has a different opinion on the current standards for word counts – and I mean EVERYONE.

So I don't see a point in making much ado about it. There are short stories – word count varies from 5,000-15,000... a novella can be anywhere between 15,000-35,000. A "short" novel, according to a reliable source (meaning someone who writes short novels and they get published) can be between 35,000-65,000 and anything over that is definitely a "novel" – with some word counts going as high as 300,000 (or possibly more).

nanowrimo

To some folks, it sounds easy to write 50,000 words... to others, it sounds impossible!

Then there are the ones who say that NaNoWriMo doesn't make authors – that it's only good for helping you develop a habit of writing regularly – and there's much more to being a published author than just writing 50,000 words.

Well, in a sense, that's partly true – there *is* much more than just writing 50,000 words. But the great folks at NaNoWriMo know this... they are quick to encourage you to "not quit" after the end of November, but to take what you've written and work on it until it's good enough to be published.

NaNoWriMo is mainly, in my own opinion, a great source to find encouragement to begin writing your novel. Everyone knows once you've finished the first draft, you still need editing, polishing, an eye-catching cover and a boatload of promotion to help you sell your book. The biggest challenge for most people is getting that first draft written.

So, if you sign up for the NaNoWriMo challenge, write your first draft during November, follow their advice to let it sit a week or two, then get back into it and edit it until it's the best you can make it... then by all means, send it off to agents or publishers. If you decide to go the Indie route, just be sure your book is ready.

Find some critique partners or beta readers who can offer some good advice before putting your novel out into the world for everyone to see. I think NaNoWriMo is an awesome adventure!

Too many people want to write, but never find the time, inspiration, or the encouragement to actually begin... NaNoWriMo is the best incentive for those who need help getting started – and although I've read plenty of reviews on why it's not helpful – I am reminded of all the participants I've met, online and in-person, who either use NaNoWriMo to write their first 50,000 words and begin a journey towards being published, or those who look forward to one month out of the year when they can ignore the mundane things that steal their time, to push themselves to once again reach for that 50,000 -word goal.

When my daughter challenged me to participate in NaNoWriMo, I had never written 1,667 words in one day – much less every day for 30 days! My daughter had just finished her first speculative novel when we participated in NaNoWriMo.

After the first time she participated, at the end of the 30 days, she had written more than 100,000 words! Each morning she would write on a Christian speculative novel until she met or passed her word count. Then each night she would write on an Amish fiction novel until she met or passed another 1,667 words for the day.

When I felt discouraged, I refused to give up,

knowing that my daughter was writing twice the words I was writing. For those who are curious, these novels have not been published – yet. While NaNoWriMo is a great incentive to write, my daughter's novels are still in the edit/ polish mode.

Although she continues to encourage others to participate in NaNoWriMo and Camp NaNoWriMo, my daughter really doesn't need the push anymore – for a year, she set a 2,000 -word daily writing goal – now her daily goal is 3,000 words.

If I had to write 3000 words each day – every day – I couldn't do it. I just couldn't think of that much to write about – at least not every day. But she does it. She's awesome!

———————— nanowrimo ————————

Once I made the decision to participate in the 30-day November challenge – to complete a 50,000 -word novel at NaNoWriMo – I needed to figure out how to begin...

First step: sign up... done.

Next step, choose who, what, when, where, why and how! Yep, I learned that in school. But it's much harder than I expected to decide what to write about – characters, plot, location, etc.

I had a chat session with my daughter, who asked me very good questions, made suggestions, and wrote down the answers. Yet when we chatted later, I surprised her when I admitted that I still wasn't sure what my novel would be about.

"I thought all that was decided," she said, confused.

I tried to explain that it was, but that now it's not working. "It doesn't seem to go anywhere in my head, so I'm guessing it's not the right choice," I told her.

Oh well, I have 30 more days to figure out how to come up with a good enough idea to write almost 1700 words every day... for the 30 days of November! How do writers come up with ideas for novels?

This is going to make for a very busy, and hopefully an exciting month, especially with Thanksgiving weekend!

Anyway, back to my story... I found myself totally unprepared for November 1, 2013. Did I create a playlist, buy snacks, plot out my genre, story line, characters, location, or choose a protagonist?

No, I did not. I didn't even plan where to write – or what to wear. I took things too literally. The instructions said not to begin before November 1... therefore I did NOTHING but sign up – and wait for November to arrive.

Don't – for Heaven's sake – follow my example!

nanowrimo

And God said, Let there be light: and there was light.

~ Genesis 1:3

Part 2

PREPARATION

CHAPTER 5

Don't Wait Until The Last Moment

As I mentioned previously, my daughter discovered a week or so before November 1st that I wasn't prepared – in time to save me from a disastrous Day 1. She threw out suggestions… I nodded my head (mostly because I wasn't really listening)… and after asking for my participant information, she went into my profile and added the information.

Unfortunately (if you remember that I wasn't really paying attention when my daughter was trying to help), when I logged into my profile page, I found a profile, a book cover and a synopsis! Wow!

If you remember the "unfortunate" comment from above, it's because it sounded like a great book – just not one I could write.

It didn't sound like me at all... Oh boy!

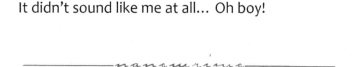

Moral of this story – don't wait until the last minute. You're allowed to write an outline, with characters, story idea and location. Then create a cover. Get it all posted on your profile page. Find some buddies. And psych yourself up – be ready!

(Of course, my daughter thinks the moral of this story is to listen to people when they're trying to help you... but I'm sure I'm not the only person who does this.)

After my auspicious beginning in November 2013, even though I hadn't done much with my novel afterwards to get it ready for publishing, I decided to participate again in November 2014... and again I wrote more than 50,000 words in 30 days – actually I wrote 60,101 words!

Even though I have written more than 50,000 words (not including the blog posts) in 30 days on two separate occasions, sometimes it still seems... and feels... impossible to do!

For the past two years, I have blogged each day

of November with my daily thoughts and word count total. These blog posts are included in this book, to hopefully be an encouragement to anyone reading them.

(Actually, I was working full-time on my job, plus writing blog posts every night, so I wrote much more than 50,000 words every day of November... but only the words in my novel counted towards my novel writing).

I also shared NaNoWriMo cartoons for part of October – and all of November. There are lots of talented people creating cartoons for the NaNoWriMo craze.

I love reading the cartoons; they make the event fun – and a laugh is always helpful when I'm struggling with my story or my word count.

This book is not only a guide of sorts, but it's meant to be an inspiration to others who want to participate in NaNoWriMo in November. I hope it's an inspiration to you.

Maybe you don't want to commit to NaNoWriMo right now; you just need a bit of encouragement because you're planning to write a novel, a novella, a short story, or just a blog post. I hope my story will be encouraging to you. We all need a helping hand at times...

If you've never participated... and if you've even thought about writing a novel... or short story... sign up! Depending on when you're reading this, it's never too early – and hopefully not too late!

But get prepared for it... there's bound to be lots of laughing, crying, eating, drinking (lots of coffee at my house, but I can't speak for others), searching (for the right word, or the right phrase), and praying!

If you're reading this in December – or during a month that's not even close to November – don't despair. Camp NaNoWriMo is held every July. It's very similar to the event in November, but the biggest difference is that you get to set your own word count goal.

I don't want to say too much about it right now, because in my opinion, the November challenge is the best idea for anyone wanting to write a novel. However, it is an option – and I talk about it in more detail in Chapter 8.

———————— nanowrimo ————————

Now that I'm an experienced NaNoWriMo participant, a month – or sometimes a week – before NaNoWriMo begins in November, I take time to write down what I want to write about. Then I begin working on a title. Once I have the title and the basic idea for the story, I send this information to my daughter, who graciously takes time out of her busy day to create a book cover for my budding novel. Unfortunately, I'm

not always gracious about it (or so I've been told)
...

A day or two after I have decided on an idea for a story and a title, when I arrive home, my daughter eagerly drags me over to her laptop to show me what she's done. While I was working at my job, she has created an amazing book cover – just for the book I plan to write!

And what does good old mom do? Ask if she can change the font... or the color... or the background... or the pictures. Just a tweak here and there...

"Hey, this looks great! Can you move my author name up a little? OK, now move it to the left a little. Good. OK."

"Wait... can you put some shadow or something, maybe a colored box, behind the title; it's hard to read... and make it just a little bigger. Yes. Good."

"Now can you do that with the author name, too? No, don't make it bigger, but maybe you could change the color again. And move it down and over to the right just a tiny bit. Well... "

"Yeah, I guess it'll do. No, I'm not trying to be difficult, but something looks off and I can't tell what it is. Can you?"

This is about the time that she tells me I'm the one who's off and she's been working on this ALL day and now I've come in and changed everything – everything! Why can't I ever like something she does without having to change it all. Which is ridiculous; I loved it, I just made a few tiny suggestions.

Oh no, there she goes again.

Is she crying... again?

Oh, man!

The problem is... if I say I love it, she doesn't believe me. She hounds me until I ask for a few changes. She always does this. The funny thing is... I ask for changes, but many times I end up going back to the original design – and I like it better than the one with the changes we just made.

This year she's doing something different... she's been teaching me how to design – hundred of layers for just one banner – or book cover. This November, even if she creates my book cover, I'll probably be the one to make the changes. Of course I'll save the original... just in case.

As I've mentioned, a week or so before NaNoWriMo began, my daughter had asked me what I was going to write about... once she had my attention, at least for a few minutes, I asked her, "Don't I have to wait until November 1st?" She assured me that most people spend weeks making plans. Oops.

A few days later, I discovered that she had been asking me questions, and had created a book idea for me, but I hadn't really been paying attention. Her ideas were great, but it didn't sound like something I could write 50,000 words about...

Who do I want to write about? What sort of location would I choose? What type of story do I want to tell? Mystery? Romance? Science Fiction?

My Christian lifestyle will help with the choosing – my goal is to write novels that are encouraging to those who will read them. If drugs, sex, immoral clothes, words or actions are part of the story, I want to show that these are bad choices with negative consequences.

As my favorite preacher says, "You can make choices, but you cannot choose the consequences." This is too true. My past is a perfect example of this. I made all the wrong choices, and suffered through the consequences of them.

That's not to say there won't be ordinary problems too... and people tend to make mistakes, bad decisions, get involved with the wrong people... so there's bound to be lots of room for just about anything to happen!

After sitting down and really giving it a lot of thought, I came up with several ideas that sounded like possible choices for my first novel...

1- poor little rich girl – this could be a great story, but I have no idea how to relate to this type of character!

2- obsessively religious husband/ father – I could write about this, but it might not the best choice just before the holiday season.

3- inept Amish teenager, unable to fit in, even among those in her family and community – is this even possible?

And the winner is...

   #3 – Amish teenager!

------------------------- nanowrimo -------------------------

Book Synopsis: Emma is not a typical Amish teenager... cooking, cleaning, sewing – everything is a challenge! Although she tries, everything she cooks is inedible – she either fails to cook it long enough to be done or it burns (picture charcoal).

Even when cleaning, Emma ends up breaking something... and every time she tries to sew or quilt, she stabs herself with a needle, makes a mess when cutting out a pattern, or finishes to discover it doesn't fit!

November 1, 2013, Emma came to life – determined to create a Christmas quilt – one that she could be proud of. How to do this was the question. Emma was no help. One way or another, Emma had to overcome her failures and succeed at something before the year – or at least the month – ends.

In all they ways acknowledge him, and he shall direct thy paths.

~ Proverbs 3:6

CHAPTER 6

Be Prepared

I cannot stress enough how important it is to be prepared. You wouldn't go on vacation without packing your swimsuit, sunblock, and your passport (if you're going out of the country).

The same thing holds for an important event like spending an entire month writing your novel. This is your time. Makes plans. Get ready. Don't go into battle unprepared!

I'm a list maker... a huge list maker. I make lists for everything! Well, maybe I didn't make a list for my first venture into the world of NaNoWriMo, but I learned from my mistake, and I have lots of good suggestions for you, if you're going to be ready in time.

First, sign up early. The first of October is a great time to begin. Just go to the official website and sign up – taking your first step to writing a novel. Don't wait. Believe me, it's better to sign up early, so you don't find yourself competing with half a million others preparing to sign up, or update their profiles, on the NaNoWriMo website.

It's free! Plus once you sign up, there's lots more to look forward to... you can meet fellow writers online and in person, get pep talks and support, track your progress, and – oh yeah – write a novel in a month.

Once you've made it to your own page, you can add all sorts of things... book title, book cover, blurb, and genre. Don't forget to add details to your own profile. Tell all about who you are and why you are participating in the challenge.

And after you log in, be sure to go look for your region – and make new friends, who you can add as buddies. I found buddies on NaNoWriMo, and I found more buddies on Twitter, Facebook, Wordpress and Google+!

When I say buddies, I don't mean have a bunch of people over to distract you; I mean those people who are also participating. They are great encouragers and a darn good support group.

Then go check out the store where you can find lots of cool stuff. I mean, of course you'll need a t-shirt, notebook, coffee mug, laptop bag and merit badge buttons, just to name a few. Oops – I forgot the posters and window clings. But the best item is the 2GB USB bracelet (but every time I check, it's sold out)!

What is that all about! How can I take NaNoWriMo seriously if I cannot purchase my 2GB USB bracelet before November 1st! Somehow I survived without it – although I'm still convinced it's the coolest item in the store.

Then it's time for snacks – lots of snacks. Be sure to get at least a few snacks that have caffeine and sugar. Writing is hard work, and it's hard to think when you feel tired... and sleepy.

If you must worry about your figure (or your health) go with healthy snacks – fruit, cheese, whole grains and lots of water! But even if you're a diabetic (which I am) you can reward yourself occasionally with a dark chocolate treat. My favorite treat isn't chocolate – it's a stone ground whole-wheat blueberry fig bar (Nature's Bakery). I buy a box at Sam's Club every month and fight my family over them...

Ha! Actually we don't fight over them. I hide 3 packs whenever we buy them (hey, they're good and that's the only way I'm assured of getting some).

———————— *nanowrimo* ————————

Another thing you can work on early is your writing playlist... we have lots of interruptions at our house, so I generally put in my earbuds when I sit down to write. Then I crank up the volume.

My playlist consists of mostly soundtracks – some slow music, some fast music, but nothing to distract me. I enjoy classical music, but much of my writing music consists of some wonderful soundtracks from movies such as The Lake House, Chronicles of Narnia, The Holiday, and a six-minute song from Superman Returns.

Now, I've never actually watched Superman Returns (matter of fact, I don't watch many movies, and we don't have cable or watch any television shows) but someone suggested this song and my daughter bought it online and added it to our playlists.

Some of my favorite gospel music to listen to is the violin solos and piano solos from The Collingsworth Family. I also have some harp music that is soothing but won't put me to sleep – so I can write.

———————— *nanowrimo* ————————

Remember, I also work a full-time job, fighting

traffic all the way there and back. When I get home, there are chores to be done and grandchildren that want a little attention. After dinner, it's time to get going on the writing, but by then I'm tired and wanting to go to bed!

Well, of course I didn't think it could be done!

But I did it…

Give instruction to a wise man, and he will be yet wiser: teach a just man, and he will increase in learning.

~ Proverbs 9:9

CHAPTER 7

Plotter or Pantser

All right, now we can explore the different ways it's been determined that most people write...

After reading more than a few articles, I discovered that there are two types of writers – plotters and pantsers. There may be more, but these are the accepted choices.

I even found, while checking the definitions, that there is an idea that everyone is essentially both – affectionately called a "plantser" – which means they utilize both ideas, but lean towards one idea more than the other. But that's just one opinion.

Then I looked up the definitions of these two words on the Internet... Of course the first definition is way off... at least when we're talking about writing. In another profession, I guess it makes sense, but let's not go there – let's stick to writing.

I tried to change it, but every time I looked for the definition, it made me giggle, so I decided I had to include it (remember, writers are crazy)…

1. Plotter – someone who secretly makes plans to do something illegal or harmful.

2. Pantser – someone who "flies by the seat of their pants," meaning they don't plan anything (or else they plan very little).

I have to admit, I've tried to be a plotter on more than one occasion – I really have – but when I sit down to write, nothing comes out the way I plotted. Sometimes when I try to stick to the plan, I sit there, in my not-so-comfortable rolling chair (the one with the back taken off in an attempt to make it a little more comfortable… but it didn't help).

I'm sitting… sitting… sitting… just sitting forever in an uncomfortable chair – with nothing to write. Literally nothing comes to mind, except how uncomfortable the chair is – and wondering *why can't I find a chair that works for me.*

Then as I'm thinking about the chair… and my shopping trip… I begin writing feverishly and eventually when I look down at it, I'm amazed because it's nothing like what I had planned to write. Well... I'm not amazed at it anymore; it's pretty much something I've come to expect.

Because – oh well. I am NOT a plotter. So why do I always start out, trying to be something I'm not. Because... uh... Well, if I knew that, maybe then I'd be a plotter. I think – think, mind you – that it's because so many people have tried to convince me that it's so much easier if I can plot out my story, with characters, community, big plots, subplots, beginning, ending, etc. Wow – that sounds good, doesn't it... if it only worked for me.

I will accept that it's much easier for those folks who are meant to be plotters – or perhaps those who have been trained to be plotters. Can you be trained to be a plotter? It's just not for me. So I'll come up with a general idea, and start writing... when the story changes, I'll go along with it, until the very end.

Okay, back to the question...

Plotter or Pantser – which are you?

First, you need to know what you're wanting to write...

fiction, non-fiction, biography, devotional, Amish, western, historical, romance...

Then, the next step is to figure out if you're a plotter or a pantser. If you don't know, that's ok. There are a vast number of articles concerning this very subject. Much more than anyone wants to read, believe me.

But if you're not sure, you might try writing down some basic facts. What do you want to write about? Once you have an idea, jot down a few characters (names, features, occupations, etc), where your story will take place, then write down the major plot points and story twists. Who is your protagonist? Your main character... comic relief...

Is there a love interest?

What do you really want to say?

The gist is – if you like to plot out everything before you begin writing, this makes you a plotter. If you'd rather jump in and start writing – without any idea at all except perhaps a basic idea – perhaps a topic and a picture in your head of the main characters, you're a pantser – you enjoy writing "by the seat of your pants". You begin writing and let the story take you wherever it goes. You're just along for the ride...

If none of the above is working for you, just sit down and begin writing – write about the first thing that comes to mind. Or better yet, I think if you're considering writing 50,000 words, you probably have a genre – and an idea – about what you want to write about.

I'm not a plotter. I'm obviously not a "pantser" either, as anyone who knows me will attest – I don't even wear pants – or shorts – or anything else that detracts from making me look – and feel – like the lady that I am. So why on earth would I want to call myself a "pantser"? I wouldn't.

If you must put a label on me, call me a *writer*!

Commit thy works unto the Lord, and thy thoughts shall be established.

~ Proverbs 16:3

CHAPTER 8

Writing Goals

You can set specific goals – or just keep up with your word count. If you write more than 1,667 words every day, you'll cross the finish line with more than 50,000 words. But if you'd like to set some goals – and celebrate when you reach each one – by all means, go ahead.

I would suggest the following:

First, set daily goals – and rewards. The daily goals need to be at least 1,667 words, which will allow you to reach 50,000 words in 30 days. Or you may consider a goal of 2,000 words – to create a cushion. For many participants, this is especially helpful in the middle if you get behind or even towards the end, to give you an extra boost to cross the finish line.

I almost hate to add this, because I want you to reach for the goal that really pushes you to write – to prepare yourself for creating a novel. But the fact is, there are other choices – and setting your own goal just might be the best option for you, especially if this is your first time participating.

Nope, not in the November challenge...

Camp NaNoWriMo is held every July – and YOU get to set your own goal. This is especially helpful for those who otherwise wouldn't participate if they really don't want to work towards a 50,000 -word goal.

It's also the perfect choice for students who want to participate, but 50,000 words is honestly too much for them, especially first time participants. My grandchildren both chose 10,000 word goals.

Honestly, neither of them reached their goal, but they were delighted with the chance to participate – and we were thrilled with the hard work they both put into their stories.

If you don't choose to work towards the 50,000 -word goal, but you still want to "win", by all means sign up and participate in July, setting a more obtainable goal. But for now, let's go back to the November goals and rewards...

A friend of mine suggested I reward myself every evening, after reaching my goal, with a 15 -20 minute walk outside to stretch your legs. My family loves walking outside after dark, with the stars shining and the crickets chirping.

I also set a goal for every 10,000 words I write... because my daughter and I are both participating, after we both reach 10,000 words we pick up pizza for the whole family to enjoy – and we rent a favorite movie to watch.

But I set extra goals!

After reaching 25,000 words, I make an appointment for a spa pedicure – just for me. If my daughter has also reached this goal, our family goes out to celebrate with a special dinner, before going back home to relax, or write more words. Sometimes I'll celebrate for no reason – except I've passed another week.

—————————— nanowrimo ——————————

It's up to you to set your goals – as few or as many as you wish. You can have as many as 10-12 goals, for starting, passing each week, passing certain word counts, and finally reaching the end – or you can have as few as one, just for starting, or for reaching 50,000 by the 30th day. Or maybe set none at all.

What am I saying! Of course you should set goals... you deserve to celebrate – and reward yourself – if you participate. My suggestion to you would be to set five goals, or if you really feel that five are too many, try setting two goals – 25,000 and 50,000 – and give yourself two big rewards when you reach these goals! Halfway through the month, if you reach 25,000 words, do something great for yourself.

I don't really know what you would consider great, but it doesn't have to be expensive or time-consuming – it needs to be something you wouldn't do for yourself without a very good reason.

Since we're talking about goals, this might be a good time to mention that most Americans celebrate Thanksgiving in November. My family does – and I wanted to take Thanksgiving Day – and the next day – off from writing.

This might be the only thing I truly planned for that first year... I told myself if I could write a few extra words each day, and my word count was more than the Friday goal, then I could take both days off without worrying about writing – and I could enjoy Thanksgiving with my family.

For 2013, my word count needed to be at least 48,300 (and for 2014, it needed to be at least 46,660). This wasn't the exact daily goal, but I figured it was close enough to put me within reach. Both years I did reach the goal, and both years I took two days off!

Final words of advice...

This is the time to write your novel... this is **NOT** the time to format, edit, or polish your words! Believe me, there will be plenty of time after this month is over to do all the other things necessary to create a book worth publishing.

Too often, people – especially ones like me – are trying to fix everything as they go. Don't do it. Just concentrate on getting your story written out. If you haven't already created a formatted document to use for your writing, don't worry about how it looks – just write your story!

Although many writers will create and upload a book cover on the NaNoWriMo site, if you haven't done so by the end of October, then wait until December. This is really not the time to do it.

Don't even think about editing the words you write – authors don't edit as they go... they really don't. Authors work hard to get their story down on paper, but many times they will set it aside for a week or two (or three).

At this point, they go back over it and do some necessary re-writing and editing. Sometimes after they finish their re-write, they will check for any errors, such as typos, grammar and punctuation (or have someone else who looks for errors).

After your novel is sold, there are several

different types of editors who will be going over your work – one for content, then one who will do a more intense line-by-line edit, and finally a proofreader who looks for typos, grammar and punctuation errors.

One more thing…

The daily word count is approximately 1,666.66667 to write 50,000 words in 30 days – so I have subtracted a few numbers most days to make the word count a little easier to remember.

The first day's goal is 1670, the second day's goal is 3335, and the third day's goal is 5000. In increments of three, I have continued adding to the next two days, and rounding off the count each third day to an even number.

For example, after three days you should have 5,000 words, 6 days is 10,000 words, 9 days is 15,000 words, 12 days is 20,000 words, 15 days is 25,000 days – adding another 5,000 words each third day until you reach the 30th days with 50,000 words.

In the next section, you'll find the blog posts that I wrote each (and every) day during November 2013 – and November 2014. A few of them have been edited just a bit when necessary, especially when there were lots of pictures on the blog post. Only one picture actually made it into the book – the one for Veterans' Day. I tried to add a few words of description to make up for the lack of pictures; otherwise a few of them made NO sense.

For example, one says, "choose… or relax, watch a Christmas show… and enjoy your long weekend!" – Imagine having to explain what's missing... I did my best.

You may be surprised to find that I was able to write more than the daily goal at times, but at many other times I lagged behind and had to work very hard to catch up. *But I did catch up. And if you get behind, you can catch up, too.*

———————— *nanowrimo* ————————

Last, but not least…

Coming up are the <u>actual</u> blog posts that I wrote and posted during November 2013 and November 2014… they're not perfect, not entertaining, they're not even necessarily interesting. What they are is the result of 30 days of writing, and my desire to communicate my feelings with other writers during the NaNoWriMo challenge.

Sometimes when I go back and read the posts, it's almost like two different people participated, the years were so different, so difficult, yet I learned much from both of them.

This experience is not for the faint of heart… it's a challenge… I'm glad I finished, but even more so, I'm glad I tried.

nanowrimo

Pray without ceasing.

~ 1 Thessalonians 5:17

Part 3

30 DAYS OF WRITING

DAY 1 – WORD COUNT GOAL: 1,670

November 1, 2013 – words written: 1,671

Today was the first day of NaNoWriMo...

I have been patiently watching and waiting for November 1st; I adamantly refused to write even the first word before it was time. I had really been looking forward to it until...

Wednesday I got sick! I won't bore you with all the details but since I'm unable to swallow much now, the sure bet is on strep throat. I know most people run to the doctor, but since I'm pretty sure that's where I got it during my scheduled visit this week, I'm not going back!

I won't kid you - it was pretty rough trying to write, but I persevered and made it! I just made it past the daily goal of 1667... my total was 1671... but I was thrilled that I was able to get that far!

I'm resting much of today, but after finishing some homemade chicken soup I'm going to get back on it. Congratulations all those who got started, and especially those who passed the goal for Day 1!

...back to my chicken soup.

nanowrimo

November 1, 2014 – words written: 1,592

Today was the 1st day of NaNoWriMo 2014! Woohoo!

Day 1 was... not long enough... not nearly long enough... for me. Being November 1, I had rent to pay and groceries to purchase...

... but I finally got settled and got going.

My total words for Day 1 might not be too impressive to some participants, but considering that I wrote 2 blogs, finished reading a book, wrote the review for the aforementioned book, ran errands, chased 2 grandchildren around while they played on their scooters and begged me to chase them, and watched "Fly Away Home" with them... twice... while writing on my novel, I didn't do too badly. I didn't quite reach the goal, but I got pretty close...

DAY 2 – WORD COUNT GOAL: 3,335

November 2, 2013 – words written: 3,377

Thank the Lord it's the weekend!

Well, it's Day 2... and I didn't spend the day writing as many others did... I spent it in bed and lying on the couch resting, sleeping a little, and whining a lot!

Ha! Just kidding. Whining is usually noisy and with my very sore throat I'm not making any sounds. My iPhone is coming in handy now. Texting doesn't force me to make any sounds... and I've also resorted to a bit of sign language, too.

Now I have the weekend to rest and get better... while keeping up with my daily writing (hopefully). I'd love any words of encouragement, especially this weekend. Keep moving forward!

---

nanourins

November 2, 2014 – words written: 3.485

I made it to Day 2! WOW!

I began early with a strange twist... My book veered off into another whole direction! My buddy suggested I keep going, so I did... and eventually it came right back to where it should be heading — so maybe I have the beginnings of another novel. I pulled the superfluous words out and saved them to another document. And it's a go!

I didn't reach the goal... I shot right passed it!

DAY 3 – WORD COUNT GOAL: 5,000

November 3, 2013 – words written: 5,000

Day 3 and I'm feeling a bit better. I think the rest, plus the warm salt water gargling, had helped.

I also participated in several writing sprints with twitter and NaNoWriMo buddies. They really helped me to push myself. This means instead of reaching the daily writing goal by midnight, I passed it at 7:21 pm and kept writing! I'm also knitting a lace scarf and doing laundry so I may not get much more writing done but that's ok! Overall it's been a good day!

———————— nanowrimo ————————

November 3, 2014 – words written: 6,003

Day 3 was a long, disturbing Monday! I had forgotten to include a short trip to Abalama so I went back and added it (for those of you not from the south, that's Alabama).

It never really seemed like I wrote very much; just the first major trip — and I'm not done with it, but with lots of interruptions and being woken an hour early this morning, I opted to quit for the night, reset the alarm and get to bed early!

Once again I passed the daily goal! Word count for day 3: I really do have 6003, although so far I keep getting an error message whenever I try to update my word count.

Day 4 – word count goal: 6,670

November 4, 2013 – words written: 5,901

Mondays… some good, some bad. I had a busy day at work; no time to think about novel, even at lunchtime. So far tonight I have met half my daily goal…

I have a confession to make.

First, I didn't really think I would succeed at NaNoWriMo – never even thought I'd write enough in a week to reach one day's goal. Now I find myself fretting because others are writing twice the daily goal (every day) while I'm finding it harder to keep up with the normal goal. I need to stop thinking about writing 4000 words a day, and find a way to be happy writing 1000-2000 words a day…

November 4, 2014 – words written: 6,673

OK… Day 4…

Yesterday (Day 3), I mentioned that I had experienced a long, disturbing Monday… well folks, I hate to be the one to break it to you, but Tuesday wasn't much better.

Once again, the day seemed "off"… and not just to me; my daughter literally said the same thing to me about her day. So we threw caution to the wind and I stopped on the way home for movies! Mom's Night Out for the adults and Charlie Brown Thanksgiving for the kids!

After enjoying our movie, we headed for the dining room table, while the kids watched Charlie Brown. We wrote a while; then we putzed around, doing some reading and catching up on the necessary social media obligations.

Social media is important – very important – to an author, but it takes a LOT of time. It's best if you stay away until the evening, or even allow yourself certain times of the day for it (but it's important to time yourself; else you'll start by checking your Facebook notifications and by the time you get off Facebook to check twitter, it'll be bedtime).

When I had written enough to pass my daily goal, I decided to quit for the night and get to bed early! Oh man, did it ever feel good! I passed the daily goal — but just barely!

DAY 5 – WORD COUNT GOAL: 8,335

November 5, 2013 – words written: 7,231

My grandchildren have recently discovered tree climbing! Every day they eagerly run outside to climb the nearby tree.

When I was their age, I loved climbing trees. I'm glad they can experience this. I love that my grandchildren would rather be outside playing, even with nothing but trees, rocks, and fresh air, than to be inside, watching television or playing electronic games! Now back to NaNoWriMo...

Today I worked at catching up to the current word count goal, but so far I'm still behind. The daily word count goal today is about 8,334 – my current word count is only 7,231.

This is way too short for my nerves, but if I don't catch up during the week, I plan to spend as much time as needed this weekend on it, hoping to pass whatever the current goal on that day...

November 5, 2014 – words written: 7,753

On Day 5, I found it getting more difficult to meet the daily goal, at least for me. Perhaps because it's Wednesday – hump day. Or perhaps because I was up at 4am and I should have tried to get to bed earlier. Or maybe it's just harder some days.

Lesson learned... weekends are good times to catch up and surge past the daily goal, by mid-week it's more difficult. The fact that I work full-time could have something to do with this – especially since it's been very hectic at work lately.

I'm curious to see if next Wednesday will be a repeat or if I'll hit my daily goal without a problem. Stay with me... I appreciate your support on this journey!

I'm quite a few words below my word count, but there's always tomorrow... or the weekend, to catch up on the 580 I'm missing, plus 1667 more for tomorrow... 1667 more for Friday... well, you get the picture.

Day 6 – word count goal: 10,000

November 6, 2013 – words written: 9,021

I took time to make a playlist with my favorite Collingsworth Family songs… I just bought their two newest CDs and the music is amazing! I'm not sure if it inspires me to write, but it certainly does inspire me! I am happy writing another 1000 words today…

Some extra writing that doesn't increase my word count was putting together Emma's family and friends. (I should have started earlier and got that done in October.)

November 6, 2014 – words written: 10,006

My original plan was to write **Life Is Not Just a Destination – It's a Journey** with my daughter. Honestly, I don't know if I can write 50,000 words or more on my own about road trips; I can't imagine coming up with enough to write 50,000 words. So… I should have chosen something else to write about…

But I don't like the idea of quitting once I've begun, so I'm just going to keep going. Who knows, I may come up with lots more road trips than I originally planned to share!

I think I can do it -- write 50,000 words -- and meet the November goal. And I only have 24 more days! I spent all evening... even though I wanted to quit around 11pm, I didn't quit. I kept going.

My daughter and I did a couple of word wars and just before midnight – I'm talking seconds... I passed the daily goal – woohoo!

Day 7 – word count goal: 11,670

November 7, 2013 – words written: 11,055

YAY! I finally spent a more productive evening – 2,034 words written today! Yes, I know I am still behind a day... but I'm much closer than I've been. AND... writing 2034 words gives me encouragement that I can catch up this weekend.

Tomorrow's total needed is 13,338... Saturday it increases to 15,000! My plan is to catch up enough tomorrow and Saturday to reach Saturday's total sometime during the day (or night). If I can, Sunday I can return to writing 1667 words per day to keep up with the daily total

---

November 7, 2014 – words written: 11,731

After catching up last night, I had high hopes of passing the daily word count today... and maybe getting a bit more ahead – for the rough times. What I didn't expect was a couple of personal calls, which took a while, replying to comments on my blog, writing another blog post plus a book review – for a really great book... plus helping someone at work with a project.

(I forgot to mention the ACFW contest I'm

participating in... 60+ pages to read and review.). But there's always tomorrow for what doesn't get done today.

Sorry – did it sound like I was whining? Nah... it's actually been a pretty cool day. And it's FRIDAY! The other good news... I did pass the daily goal – I really did!

Woohoo!

WEEK 1 – First Week Finished

Honestly, as I copied my first week's writing adventures for both years 2013 and 2014, it was quite embarrassing…

I'm not writing this book to brag, or to show you how easy it is… it is NOT easy. But it is very satisfying to participate and show yourself just how well you can do. If you get behind, don't give up!

In 2013, I got behind on days 4, 5, 6 and 7. In 2014, I started out behind on days 1 and 2, but caught up by day 3, then got behind on day 5, but caught up again on day 6.

Just as important, if you get ahead, don't quit trying to write at least 1600 words each day – believe me, it's too easy to get ahead for a few days, then find yourself way behind.

I hope sharing my experiences will encourage you to participate – and to do your best to keep up with the daily goals.

If you do so, you'll find yourself finishing the month of November quickly – and ready to begin editing your story for publishing.

All right, let's move on to Week Two…

———————— nanowrimo ————————

Day 8 – word count goal: 13,335

November 8, 2013 – words written: 13,262

Ok, Day 8… I wrote my post, but lost it somehow. So even though it's late, I'm doing it again.

Yay! It's Friday!

Burgers and fries tonight with plenty of writing time… or so I thought. Unfortunately the kids did not cooperate. So seriously, writing did not begin until 11:10 and I stopped a little past midnight. 1207 words in an hour was great. Now if I could figure out how to write for several hours a day I could stay caught up to my goal!

Tomorrow is a huge NaNo Write-in… to get word count up. See you there!

———————— nanowrimo ————————

November 8, 2014 – words written: 13,401

Today has been very busy…

I signed up to judge two categories in the ACFW First Impressions contest. I have read all ten of the samples. Today I finished scoring one category; now I just need to finish the other category and this job is done.

We've been writing... editing... planning...

I have several novels to finish reading so I can post reviews for them; planning to complete at least one more tomorrow.

My novel writing works well if I begin early in the morning; take breaks to do other things, returning to it at different times to write. So far, this has worked well enough to keep me up-to-date on the all-important daily word count goal.

Once again, I wrote enough to pass the daily goal. Whew!

DAY 9 – WORD COUNT GOAL: 15,000

November 9, 2013 – words written: 15,000

Today is the famous November 9 Writing Marathon Day for everyone signed up to write 50,000 words in the 30 days of November!

You probably won't be surprised by this post… you can guess what happens when you make plans to attend a writing marathon… especially one which has been planned and publicized by all who are following NaNoWriMo.

Our local group met at the nearby mall; the idea was to move to a different location in the mall every hour. My grandchildren are also writing in the Young Writers Program – so they were going with us. We stopped to pick up a few supplies, then got to the mall and looked for our group.

They were all at one long table at the food court. Half of them were eating lunch; some were chatting, some surfing the Internet, and two or three were writing. We ordered food and sat down. By the time we finished lunch and began writing, the group decided to move. Yep, it was about time.

So we all headed upstairs. Then we were told we couldn't stay together there because we were blocking too much of the hallway. So everyone spread out, sat down against a wall, and began to write (except those who were socializing).

After about 30 minutes, I headed back downstairs to find a restroom. My family quickly caught up with me... to ask if we could make other plans. We did... we tried a local fast food restaurant, but their electrical outlets were covered (and we needed to recharge laptops), so we headed home.

When we got home, we all discovered the most anyone had written was just a little over 100 words! Not much of a writing marathon, huh? So now we're back to sitting at home, writing at the table.

Oh well, back to writing 1000 words every evening. At this rate, I will have 40,000 words by the end of November. Not something to be ashamed of; I think that's something to be proud of. So what if it isn't NaNoWriMo's goal and I'm not a NaNo Winner. I've decided to be happy with myself, no matter what my word count is on November 30th...

I'm not asking anyone else to stop doing NaNoWriMo... and I intend to keep blogging every day until the end of November. And I don't mean to sound discouraging or critical. I intend to give it as much time and work as I have for these nine days.

MY GOAL: to write every day until the end of November! You can still see my word count each time you visit my blog… just look for the box at the top right, next to my current post.

―――――――――― nanowrimo ――――――――

November 9, 2014 – words written: 13,401

Today has been very busy…

The most important work today has been editing A Mother For Leah. As a critique partner and editor, this is something I take very seriously. We've been editing… trying new recipes for another project… and editing.

There are a lot of changes; it is taking a long time, but we continue, not giving up. The writing of my novel for November is less important; therefore, I did not add words today.

My novel writing will continue tomorrow, after the editing is complete. I have even taken extra time off from my other duties to be able to finish this.

DAY 10 – WORD COUNT GOAL: 16,670

November 10, 2013 – words written: 16,602

It's Sunday afternoon in Tennessee! The sun is shining and it's a beautiful day. My daughter and I took the grandchildren to McDonald's for lunch and to play on the "Touch 2 Play" computer games. (We snuck in a burger and chicken sandwich from Wendy's for the adults). The kids have eaten, and are happily playing... allowing us to write. After I finish this post, I will be writing on my novel.

Since my attempt at the much-lauded November 9th NaNoWriMo Writing Marathon Day didn't go as planned, I decided to stay up late, then get up early and do my own WRITING MARATHON today with my daughter and grandchildren.

Last night I worked hard to make up for not getting much writing done and stayed up til 2am writing... I wrote 1739 words all together, even if they didn't all count because 800 were written after midnight!

Today I have written my 1667 words... and I'm hard at work to catch up to the Day 10 goal of 16,667. At the moment, my word count is 13,704 – so all I need to pass the daily word goal is 2,964 words!

I might not get 2,964 more words today, but I'm

pretty confident I can get at least half that. If I do, tomorrow I would need to write 3,149 just to achieve the Day 11 goal.

However, after that it's back to work during the daytime. And I've had a lot of trouble getting my 1667 words at night when I come home. Hopefully... if I can catch up today and tomorrow, the nightly writing will go a bit easier. Otherwise, it's back to playing catch-up each weekend.

NOW... isn't it funny how discouraged I was yesterday about the 50,000 -word count, but today I'm thinking I can do it, so I'm encouraged?

Well, I stand by what I said yesterday; the most important thing isn't reaching the 50,000 words by the end of November, the most important thing is to try... and to not give up. That said, if I don't reach 50,000 words by the end of November, I will still be glad I finished the challenge. And taking the challenge has already helped me to accept the decision to write a non-fiction book once November is over!

———————————— nanowrimo ————————————

November 10, 2014 – words written: 16,704

I took the day off from work to enjoy an extra day with my wonderful family! Much of the day was spent editing A Mother For Leah... but there was still plenty of family time, too. And it was a lovely day! And I wrote enough to pass the daily goal...

Day 11 — word count goal: 18,335

November 11, 2013 – words written: 18,400

My blog tonight is dedicated to all those who put their lives on the line to protect our freedoms!

Thank you to all our military personnel for the sacrifices you have made for our freedom.

Happy Veteran's Day!

Our servicemen deserve our
1. prayers
2. respect
3. Support

November 11, 2014 – words written: 17,002

Our family is requesting prayers for our extended family in Georgia.

Cameron Miller said his goodbyes to his family and early this morning was carried up to Heaven, leaving behind disease, blindness, pain and suffering. Those left behind are going to miss him; we will grieve his early passing... but our grief will be eased because we know he's now patiently waiting to be reunited with his loved ones.

DAY 12 – WORD COUNT GOAL: 20,000

November 12, 2013 – words written: 20,000

It was a cool 54 degrees this morning... by the time I got to work it was a chilly 46 degrees... and a cold 34 degrees this evening on the way home!

Winter is definitely on its way!

NaNoWriMo is going well. My daughter attended her first write-in tonight and it was very successful. She won the first WORD WAR – coming in at 658 words in 15 minutes! Woohoo!

My friend would probably have 40,000 by now, except she insists on editing and writing just as if she were writing any other time. She is the true form of "author" to me. I was blessed to read an advanced copy of her first novel and it was terrific. So far, no one has offered to publish it – they have no idea what they're missing out on!

Today at work was a typical Monday... tons of work, crazy phone calls, etc. I'm glad it's over and tomorrow is Wednesday – which means we're halfway to the weekend.

I'm going to say goodnight early, so I can get the other 1000 words I really want to work towards tonight.

nanowrimo

November 12, 2014 – words written: 20,419

As much as I want to complete NaNoWriMo and November with 50,000 words -- and a rough draft of a new novel -- I'm not sure I can do it this year. Last year the month was pretty much the same as previous months, and all I had to do was spend hours each day writing.

This year, the month is full of difficulties -- new job, new city, new home, new problems. Friday and Saturday we'll be spending 10-12 hours or more on the road -- a family commitment we just can't miss.

So... I'm not giving up. I will keep writing... keep trying... until December 1st.

Day 13 — word count goal: 21,670

November 13, 2013 — words written: 21,735

I have just encountered something I never thought I'd see... yesterday I got to the 'end' of my novel, with a whopping 20,000 words (so obviously I'm not done). But it certainly read like it would be a great ending, so maybe it could be the end, which means I need to add 30,000-40,000 more words between the beginning and this great end.

My daughter and I had chatted about possible plots, etc. when we first began writing in November and when asked, she mentioned a few ideas to put in my novel. Reading through the ideas yesterday, I crossed off a couple I had already added.

I liked one idea, although I had already written about it. But I kept thinking about it, along with other ideas and after awhile, I was ready to begin writing again. The story was going great, a possible romance in the future was even hinted at, and then...

'HE' showed up.

One thing you probably need to know... I'm not writing an action, mystery, or horror novel. I'm writing a wholesome, decent novel about an Amish family. So when a character shows up, ready (and planning) to do harm... well, let me just say I was more than surprised... I was shocked (considering I'm writing it).

I didn't know characters could just pop into your novel and make themselves at home, doing whatever they want. I mean Who's writing this thing, anyway!

When I finally let my daughter read it last night, she said, "Ok mom, now I know you're really an AUTHOR. If you weren't, that would never happen. So all right, tonight after work, it's back to work on the novel... apparently, it's not mine anymore – it belongs to the characters.

I sure hope they finish it before the deadline...

———————— *nanowrimo* ————————

November 13, 2014 – words written: 22,002

This week has been more difficult, since my step grandson died on Tuesday. Now we're preparing to travel to Georgia this weekend. Working very hard to get word count tonight...

On the other hand, the writing is going much better than I expected – especially considering where my mind has been this week. I've caught up and moved past... Word count looks great!

Day 14 – word count goal: 23,335

November 14, 2013 – words written: 23,385

Day 14 is almost half done. And the cool part is that I'm almost half done too, with my novel. At the moment, my word count is 22,004 and I have tonight and tomorrow to complete another 3,000 words (+ 22,004) = 25,000 big ones!

Yes I know there are over-achievers out there who are done… or will be by tomorrow night (the halfway point), but having never done this before I'm just thankful that I'm still in the game!

You remember last week, don't you… when I kept saying I was going to catch up soon. Well, unlike most who are participating, I had more trouble last week – thankfully this week has been easier.

I think it's because I really didn't know what I was doing last week (of course, this week I'm not much better, but it seems to be working out okay). And of course last week I thought I was going to have to figure out everything I was going to write down to create my novel.

Uh uh… not so…

This week I decided to start another chapter – with what I thought would be a minor scene. After writing a page or so, suddenly this dark villain shows up! Honest, he hadn't even entered my mind until I was almost done with the scene... then

BOOM!

There he was... so I kept writing and although I admit I wasn't too comfortable with him, it worked out pretty good. I'm getting back in touch with him tonight and I'm determined to have my way with him!

he might be considering harm...

he might have already done harm...

... but he won't get away with it!

and killing is strictly **banned**!

Well, at least I hope so – but he's mean... who knows what he might do next... I'd better finish my lunch and get back to work so I can go home and see what happens next... I never expected so many surprises.

November 14, 2014 – words written: 24,010

Novel going great... I think it's easier today to write... and try to put this weekend out of my mind for now. Instead of leaving tonight, we've decided to leave around 6am and drive straight down to Winder.

I'm going to keep writing as long as I can... if my word count gets very high, I plan to stop posting my word count tonight and post the rest of it after midnight – for tomorrow's word count, since I'll be out of town and most definitely NOT writing.

WEEK 2 – Halfway There

I sure hope you're still with me... if you've gotten behind, now is the time to catch up!

I found weekends especially helpful for getting my word count past the daily goal... and sometimes even more. I hope you're not behind, but if you are, schedule some extra time during the next weekend and try to catch up – or get ahead a bit.

Another thing I've noticed... is that when the writing is going well, I tend to write much less in my blog post – sometimes just a short paragraph - but when the story writing is going slow, my blog post is much bigger! I guess this means I have lots more time to write a blog post if my writing is dragging along, but less time to write a blog post when the book writing is going well. Oh well...

All right, let's move on to Week Three...

nancurine

Day 15 – word count goal: 25,000

November 15, 2013 – words written: 25,000

Woo hoo! I made it halfway! Check out this senior lady's word count…

Did I ever tell you why I signed up to write a novel in the 30 days of November…

Well, I kept seeing/ hearing things for months … to tempt me to join. When I mentioned the idea to my daughter, she said she had thought about joining in previous years, but had been too busy with other things. Then she said if I wanted to sign up, she would, too. Oh boy, that did it. After all, she might miss out if I didn't sign up, right?

So I did… and she did…

My daughter is very talented and she is doing great. And she's been a huge help with encouragement and ideas. Unfortunately I might have hurt her feelings a bit when I didn't take any of her ideas at first; but it was because I was just talking… not really listening to anything I said, but she wrote it all down and expected me to do it. Are you kidding me? I couldn't even remember ever saying most of it!

Anyway (not anywho or anyways – but anyway) it is going very well. I never knew I would have so much fun writing a novel in 30 days – well, who knew!

... certainly not me.

We both attended the MEET & GREET on October 28th; then we went to a KNOX QUEST all day writing marathon on November 9th. And my daughter went to a write-in a few days ago and got a really cool sticker for winning a WORD WAR session. She said this was the best one yet, because everyone was really serious about writing and she got 3000+ words written (plus the cool sticker).

After last weekend was a bust for both of us (as far as writing goes), my daughter called and got a room for a write-in... yep, we're all meeting at Chick Fil A tonight for WORD WARS and to write...

and write...

and WRITE...

---

nanowrimo

November 15, 2014 – words written: 25,001

I wrote until late in the night to make my word count, but now it's time to put everything away and get a little sleep, before heading down to Georgia for the funeral...

Prayers are appreciated, dear friends.

Day 16 – word count goal: 26,670

November 16, 2013 – words written: 26,681

Am I high maintenance?

It's Day 16... I have passed the daily goal again, but I want to rant a bit, is that ok? I was very excited about joining NaNoWriMo this year – it is my first year. I jumped in with both feet, hoping for the best.

Wanting to do everything I could to succeed, I joined the local WriMo group. But instead of being encouraged, I always come away discouraged.

I have taken my family to the "family friendly" meetings. Everyone in my family is signed up with NaNoWriMo so we're all writing – even the kids. But we always leave the meetings soon after arriving because...

What do you do when the adults are walking around and talking loud, making it hard to write... but the people at nearby tables keep making comments about kids not belonging at the meetings, where writers are trying to bring up their word count.

Hello... the adults are the ones who are being disruptive. The kids are sitting quietly, writing.

It is pretty obvious that the atmosphere is not

friendly to families... We tried at the first meeting. We tried at the November 9th gathering at the mall (talk about loud and disruptive... whew). We tried tonight.

We give up. We will have our own meetings, with word wars and prizes and treats. We will stop feeling discouraged. We will make it to the end.

By the way, the two meetings (the one tonight and the one on November 9th) were especially for those who were behind but want to catch up their word count to the daily word count goal... this does not apply to any of us, as we are ahead of the daily goal... we just wanted a little socialization with others doing the challenge, but I get more encouragement from those who respond and reply to my daily blogs.

Okay, so if you just read the above paragraph, you know I really want encouragement and response from others doing the challenge – through this blog. For all those who have already responded to my blog,

THANK YOU! and GOD BLESS YOU!

---

nanowrimo

November 16, 2014 – words written: 27,614

We barely made it home – mostly by the grace of GOD. My daughter read to me, I sang...

talked... hummed... anything to stay alert. We passed one vehicle down in the ditch between the Interstate lanes. I have no idea which way the vehicle was heading – the driver had probably fallen asleep at the wheel... it only takes a moment.

OK! Still writing... I've met my goal, so I'm just going on and on... I'm about a thousand ahead now, so I'm going to stop for today and get to bed early.

Day 17 – word count goal: 28,335

November 17, 2013 – words written: 28,410

Day 17 has been long and tough!

It started out fine, but my daughter wasn't feeling well. By mid afternoon she was down for the count! It looks like FLU to me.

Unfortunately, as a child I taught her to share... just kidding – I sure hope she keeps it to herself but in a day or two we could have a home with 4 sick, whiny individuals.

I took advantage when she was snoozing to write – not a lot, but past the daily goal anyway. I wanted to get a little ahead but perhaps I can tomorrow.

We would certainly appreciate your prayers.

———————————— *nanowrimo* ————————————

November 17, 2014 – words written: 29,121

Shhh... don't tell anyone, but I got a lot of plotting done at work today. Everyone is gone – either on vacation or to training, so I had lots of extra time.

Sometimes I wonder if anything I'm writing is worth keeping! However, I know the basic rule of NaNoWriMo... don't edit – write!

It doesn't matter how good or bad it is... keep writing. Get done, then next month come back and read over it... then decide what to keep and what to throw out! LOL

Plugging along... trying to get so far past my goal that I can quit early if I need to!

Day 18 – word count goal: 30,000

November 18, 2013 – words written: 30,062

… 12 more days of nanowrimo

Good morning, Monday…

Either one works today. I'm happy to say my daughter is hanging in there; I'm even happier to say I'm still well. I don't mean to sound horrible, but I do have to work outside the home.

But I did get up early, shower and eat breakfast, then got fresh water, meds, etc for the sick widdle girl. She's texted a few times, so we're keeping in contact.

I sure hope she feels better tonight and is able to write some – she hates getting behind even more than I do! Thanks for all your well wishes and prayers. Take care and I'll be back tomorrow.

—————————— nanowrimo ——————————

November 18, 2014 – words written: 32,044

Today was very productive at work… interviews and unexpected news… causing a lot of work to catch up to where we were last week!

No time for writing — none — but at home I got

a lot more writing done. I've practically been writing the entire time I've been home tonight, and I'm feeling very productive in my writing, too!

Occasionally my book veers off into another genre, but I gently pull it back! Actually, what I do is save it to a different file name, then come back and remove all the superfluous thoughts… then get right back into it. And although I work hard to do so, I have a feeling once I'm done and begin editing, my book is going to quickly be whittled down to about half what it will be on November 30th!

That's ok… I only need to keep what's really meant to be in the book anyway – right?

DAY 19 – WORD COUNT GOAL: 31,670

November 19, 2013 – words written: 31,729

Mondays have never been my favorite day, and yesterday was no exception. My daughter was sick with stomach flu, I felt pretty awful at times, too… and was afraid I had caught it from her over the weekend.

And the day seemed so long… but Mondays are often like that.

Last night I thought I would never get past my daily word count. I only got one green bar, because I did get just past 30,000 words but not 1,667 daily words – oh well.

OK, it's Tuesday now and time to stop whining!

I'm getting my blog post done on my break, so at lunchtime maybe – just maybe I can do some work on my novel. One of the problems I faced last night was lack of Amish names… I had challenged my daughter to a WORD WAR so in order not to stop writing, I had to type, "and Mr. NAME went to the door…", "I'm not sure, NAME, what to do now."

You see where I was going… the longer the novel gets, the more names I need and I'm using lots of duplicate names because it seems to be the way it really is… so I'm also needing to keep all the Samuels and Rachels and Henrys sorted. That's the first thing I'm going to do today... make sure I have all the spots where I need a new name filled.

It's a dirty job... but somebody's gotta do it.

nanowrimo

November 19, 2014 – words written: 33,817

Hump Day... I don't care much for that term, but I love Wednesdays — because there's only 2 more days until the weekend!

Now, I'd love to stay and chat... but I have a book review to finish, so I must get my work done and get some sleep!!!

Day 20 – word count goal: 33,335

November 20, 2013 – words written: 33,396

DAY 20 – I can't believe I made it this far!

I mentioned to my daughter this morning that we are two-thirds done with the challenge tonight. Only 10 more days to go… YAY!

I realize my novel might not be done by November 30, but I am confident that I will finish it. What I want to complete first is… the challenge of writing 50,000 words in 30 days (or less). This was the big challenge for me – to actually stop procrastinating and get the book started. 50,000 words is a great start!

I remember the last week of October… I was so panicked, trying to figure out how to begin, what to say, what to do, etc. I finally got an idea of what I wanted to write about, then I was stuck on who! where! when!

I'm just glad I had no idea in October how many characters I would need to write a novel. Keeping track of them has been harder than I would have imagined, considering they're my creation – my characters.

My daughter has had stomach flu since last Saturday night, so we are all trying to juggle chores and cooking and writing… she began to feel better last night and started working on catching up to the daily goal. She didn't make it, but I think she just might do it today! She is a terrific writer and can write twice the words I do when we do a timed WORD WAR.

It hasn't been easy for me to keep up with my daily goals, but so far I'm just keeping barely ahead – but that's enough for now. My hope is to get ahead enough to pass the 50,000 goal by November 27th and keep going until the novel is finished.

I am on my way out to pick up my lunch. My favorite treat is veggie-fried rice (there are lots of vegetables and it isn't greasy like some I've had in the past).

The week is half over now... let's push on towards the weekend!

November 20, 2014 – words written: 36,013

November 20th... only 10 more days to write furiously, trying to reach that much-coveted goal of 50,000 words! I'm getting much closer! I'm at 36,000 and that's more than the daily goal of 33,340 — give or take a few words.

This book is my baby... but I'm sharing it. Once

I'm done with the first draft, I plan to spend much of December editing it. Then I'm turning it over to my daughter, who will add her thoughts to it. Then we'll do another edit — together.

We're getting closer and closer to the idea of self-publishing... I'm not convinced yet that I want this book to be self-published, but I'm getting easier with the thought that it mostly likely will be self-pubbed, if I want to see it published!

I mean, who wants to read about a 50-something grandmother who's afraid to drive farther than 30 minutes from home... but finally does just that — my first vacation in many, many years — and I pick a place 7+ hours from home... and lived to tell about it!

... ok... maybe someone just might want to read about it.

Day 21 – word count goal: 35,000

November 21, 2013 – words written: 35,103

When I look at this picture, I think of Christmas... we live in East Tennessee, where it rarely snows, to the great disappointment of my grandchildren. Well, actually my daughter and I both love watching it snow, too.

We always planned someday to move where we could enjoy the snow in the winter, but so far, it's just a dream.

There are so many possibilities for those who really want snow... Alaska, Wisconsin, Maine – how do you pick? (besides the obvious... you go where you have a job).

We laugh about moving somewhere just for the snow, only to find that it stops snowing there. So we have revisited our dream.

The new dream is to move closer to North Carolina, Virginia, or Kentucky. To not go specifically for more snow, but a few cooler degrees (especially in summer). Then to plan vacations around Christmas and go somewhere just for the snow!

Will we do it? Possibly. At least it seems more doable than the previous plans.

I'll keep you posted.

In the meantime, everyone seems to be on the mend, and we're writing... writing... writing.

9 more days!

———————————— *nanowrimo* ————————————

November 21, 2014 – words written: 38,917

Today has been great! I'm doing so well, I'm changing my goal — to 55,000!

WEEK 3 – You Can Do It

Will my NaNoWriMo novel be inspired?

For me, it's an absolute must! Because I feel that God is leading me to do this. I'm praying that He uses me to write something inspirational that someone else needs to hear... to read.

I know that I am not worthy; I've made a mess of my life again and again. But maybe... just maybe He might use me to speak to someone else.

And maybe while speaking to you, I might learn more, too.

———————— nanowrimo ————————

Day 22 – word count goal: 36,670

November 22, 2013 – words written: 36,770

The days are passing quickly... day 22 is almost gone (or it will be by the time I get off work and take my family out to dinner, stop for snacks and head back home) – I may have a couple of hours to write!

The accumulated daily goal for Day 21 was 35,000... I just passed the goal in time to hurriedly shower and fall into bed, exhausted.

Yesterday my plan was to write an extra 1000 words – HA! Instead, I found myself going back to the beginning of the novel and filling in gaps. I don't think we're supposed to do that now, it might be considered editing, but it worked out ok for me, since I did reach the goal and pass it ever so slightly.

And tonight... tomorrow... Sunday...

So far, weekends have been my worst time to write – the first weekend I got behind and last weekend I barely got caught up, but I've stayed caught up all week, so perhaps this weekend I will forge ahead.

My goal is to get all 15,000 words written by Monday or Tuesday and pass the 50,000 mark. Once I'm officially declared a winner, then I can go back and fill in more gaps and do some serious editing.

Will I write 15,000 in 72-96 hours... who knows?

---

nanowrimo

November 22, 2014 – words written: 42,002

WOOHOO! Most NaNoWriMos are trying to reach... or move past 36,667... I just passed 42,000!

I LOVE SATURDAYS!!!

If I just write 1,667 words every day through November 30th, I'll pass 55,000 (my new goal)... today has been such a great time for writing!

PLUS I read the two books for the featured author this week, plus one for BookLook Bloggers, plus two for friends... and reviewed all of them! Whew!

Day 23 – word count goal: 38,335

November 23, 2013 – words written: 38,401

Just as we have experienced in previous weeks, we get less writing done on the weekend.

Today was no exception. Just squeaked by with required goal...

I was blessed to spend an hour chatting with a close friend tonight... she and her daughters participated in a holiday bazaar today. In her words:

We had the bazaar today... Several things were just plain sold out and our friend sold many, many aprons and rice packs. Ashley made doll clothes for the 18" dolls and she sold every single outfit. Clara made some suet bird feeders and they all sold as well. I made some snowmen that had 3 flavors of popcorn seasoning inside. These too sold out. It was a good day.

I'm happy for my friend... she is teaching her daughters well and they are very talented.

We had a great time chatting.

It's getting late so I'm off to bed.

November 23, 2014 – words written: 45,111

Well, while I'm 5,000 words ahead of the daily goal, I'm just keeping up today... so I'm not going to change my goal again — at least not yet. I'm not sure how many words I can get over the holidays.

At least I'm pretty sure I can reach the main goal of 50,000... any more will be "pure gravy"... and an easier time finishing the book, I hope.

DAY 24 – WORD COUNT GOAL: 40,000

November 24, 2013 – words written: 40,035

Another busy Sunday has kept me from writing. After getting some much-needed chores done this afternoon, and doing a bit of experimenting on a new dessert, I'm ready to write...

Oh yeah, the dessert? I have tried for years to make a dessert that my parents would bring to me for Christmas, but it never worked out. So today I've created my own... with lime jello, cream cheese, whipped topping (we make fresh because we can't use cool whip (it has high fructose corn syrup in it), crushed pineapple, miniature marshmallows and nuts (but I didn't add nuts yet). It is chilling but should be ready to eat sometime tonight.

So now it's back to writing. TIme to get serious... no more posting... or twitter... or facebook... or anything else that might deter me from my daily goal.

See ya tomorrow... and God bless you.

November 24, 2014 – words written: 47,994

Oh my goodness! I'm so close! Last year at this time I think I had about 42,000 or so... and going crazy trying to find the time to write!

Even with sickness, death, vehicle issues, work issues, etc. it has went much smoother this year; I'm glad I signed up... and stuck with it.

DAY 25 – WORD COUNT GOAL: 41,670

November 25, 2013 – words written: 41,710

It is Day 25 and I'm still rushing to keep up with the daily goal... yesterday's was 40,000 and I barely made it – again.

Today it's 41,667 and that really doesn't look like much more than the previous goal, but since lately all I worry about is catching up, staying caught up, and getting ahead so that I don't get behind...

I'm ready to QUIT !!!

but I won't... at least not yet.

OK, let's change the subject for a minute...

My family recently visited Cracker Barrel and by the time we left, we had been talked into coming back for Thanksgiving. Since we are a small family, we have decided to let them do the cooking and we will just enjoy the day!

Yum... turkey, cornbread dressing, sugar-cured ham, sweet potato casserole, cranberry relish and a slice of pumpkin pecan streusel pie with real whipped cream!

Happy Thanksgiving. God bless you.

———————— nanowrimo ————————

November 25, 2014 – words written: 50,000

50,000 words written!

TA DA . . .

Done. Finished. Over.

Day 26 – word count goal: 43,335

November 26, 2013 – words written: 43,340

Hello World! Sometimes I forget you're out there because it's...

Day 26 of NaNoWriMo!

and that's the world I've lived in for the past 26 days...

But if you glance at the little box on the right that shows my total number of words... I'm still in the ballgame, with 43,000 words. I just have to write 400 more words tonight to be caught up... I'm planning to write at least 1400 more words!

My plan is to stay as far ahead as I can and to get those 50k words done so I can be declared a WINNER! Then I plan to spend most of December finishing the novel and taking a break. I've read that it is important to finish the book and take at least 2 weeks off, without reading or doing anything to it, so...

January 15th... time for major editing.

In the meantime, yes I'm writing on my lunchbreak again... iPhones come in handy for times when you need to get something done online.

———————————— *nanourimo* ————————————

November 26, 2014 – words written: 52,483

OKAY — I know I wrote my 50,000 words... but I reset my goal to 55,000, so I'm still writing! It's getting close to an end, but I think I can still get it past 55,000.

I think I can... I hope I can...

DAY 27 – WORD COUNT GOAL: 45,000

November 27, 2013 – words written: 45,010

What is it about weekends, holidays and extra time off…

We have so many things to do that we stay out longer and I get less and less writing done! Today, for example, we left home early to go to the grandchildren's piano lessons – actually we didn't have a piano lesson today, we had breakfast (homemade waffles) with our friend, who happens to be the piano teacher. We left there at 11:30am, ran by a local shop nearby and found two inexpensive (not necessarily cheap… but they were) violins for the grandchildren to learn to play. It was 12:30…

We headed back to the teacher's house so she could check them out. She said the violins would work and she kept them to clean up, replace strings, and do a little more maintenance. She is a wonderful friend, pianist, violinist… and composer.

By this time it was 1:30pm… we went to Wendy's for crispy chicken sandwiches (nuggets for my grandson). Time: 2:15pm

From there it was just a hop, skip and a jump to Cracker Barrel to pick up our Thanksgiving meal, packaged nicely in a big box… and then we figured a quick trip to the mall to check out Williams Sonoma for pumpkin pecan butter would be a good idea. They were on sale for $8.99 so we bought 4, as they usually last us awhile. Time: 4pm

Then it was time to run by a Redbox to return the movie I rented last night... but of course I forgot and got almost home, then had to turn around and go back.

By the time we got home, it was almost 6:00pm. Empty car. Fix dinner (we snacked on a little of the Thanksgiving food). Grandchildren settled. Friend in Washington State called to chat.

Now it's after 8pm and I'm writing my blog.

Hey, after it's done maybe I can write on my novel... what a "novel" idea!

I'm thankful for a day spent with my family, visiting with a friend, finding two affordable violins, and that we arrived back home safely, so it was a good day! Now I'm really going to get to my novel writing...

November 27, 2014 – words written: 54,000

Today is the 27th day of NaNoWriMo 2014!

I hope all my readers have a blessed Thanksgiving!

DAY 28 – WORD COUNT GOAL: 46,607

November 28, 2013 – words written: 46,679

Happy Thanksgiving!

This is a day to remind us all to be thankful…

My home-schooled grandchildren created a harvest tree with fall decorations and leaves that have notes, telling what our family is thankful for…

GOD's love, family, Tom & Joyce Harmon (special friends) and SNOW!

I have so much to be thankful for… my salvation and the love God showed me (that I don't deserve and at times have not appreciated), my wonderful family, including 2 very loving grandchildren, my home and my job, friends who are encouraging and supportive, music – which is important to everyone in our home, IBLP, ATI and Bill Gothard, who have made such a difference in our home and our lives… and all the many blessings in my life.

And it is Day 28 for those busy with the NaNoWriMo challenge!

TWO NaNoWriMo buddies of mine have passed the 50,000 mark and were declared a WINNER!

Mike Coville and **JC Morrows** – **CONGRATULATIONS**!

It is also the weekend to catch all those amazing sales, so my post will be short... I'm on my way out to shop!

November 28, 2014 – words written: 55,208

Today is the 28th day of NaNoWriMo 2014!

Choose... writing, shopping (after all, the best sales are Thanksgiving weekend), or relax, watch a Christmas show... and enjoy your long weekend!

Day 29 – word count goal: 48,335

November 29, 2013 – words written: 50,310 (just before midnight)

Big day today... Day 29 of NaNoWriMo...

As far as NaNoWriMo goes, I still haven't passed 50k but I feel that I am a winner nonetheless, because I accepted the challenge, I wrote every day for a month, I started a novel, I participated in local events, and I kept up every day (for the most part) with the daily goal. Even if someone doesn't pass the 50k mark to be declared an official winner by NaNoWriMo, shouldn't they be considered a winner, just for trying?

However, unless I get very sick or my laptop dies, I should be able to pass the 50k mark tomorrow before the deadline! YAY!

OK, it's back to writing...

PS – I have received SO MANY encouraging comments... especially tonight!

I DID IT! I completed the 50,000 -word challenge on November 29th... actual validated count is 50,310!

And my daughter validated her word count at 50,291 an hour before I did, and was declared a WINNER, too! Congratulations, Rachel!

---------------*nanowrimo*---------------

November 29, 2014 – words written: 58,515

I didn't want to write posts with totals during the past few days, but in case you are wondering, here are the daily totals...

I have one more day... my original goal was to pass 50,000... then to pass 55,000... now I think I can get past 60,000!

YOU CAN DO IT!

DAY 30 – WORD COUNT GOAL: 50,000

November 30, 2013 – words written: 50,310

Today our family will celebrate! Lunch is planned... hopefully I can think of someplace special... then we will just spend time together (and no writing allowed)...

Of course, tonight I will get back into my novel and work a little more... although I wrote the ending, it needs more work... more words... more time.

I am planning to take a 2-week break when I feel that I am done. Then go back to it and see what I think... I'm sure more editing will be done.

But with God's help, if it is His will, I will be thinking seriously of looking at publishing choices. And while I was writing this month, God gave me an idea for another novel that I will be starting next year.

God bless you... And a special blessing to those who prayed and encouraged me. You are the best! Please keep following my blog... I'll keep writing...

nanowrimo

November 30, 2014 – words written: 60,101

Today is the LAST DAY!

I hope those of you who are still working towards the 50,000 –word goal reach it in time. But if you don't… it doesn't mean anything except that you didn't reach 50,000 words.

If you participated, you won… because it doesn't matter how far you get… as long as you try… as long as you tried.

I'm done. I'm stopping now.

WEEK 4 – You Made It

No more pep talks… no more banter… no more posts.

YOU DID IT.

30 days… over.

Time to relax… and celebrate.

———————————— nanowrimo ————————————

Part 4

FINAL RESULTS

CHAPTER 9

Congratulations

If you <u>participated</u> in NaNoWriMo... Congratulations! You don't have to write 50,000 words to be a winner! Yes, people who reach the 50,000 –word mark are excited – and they deserve to feel so. But if you did your best – your very best – you can congratulate yourself for a job well done – no matter what your final word total may be.

Confession time... I didn't sign up for NaNoWriMo, hoping to write 50,000 words in 30 days. I really didn't. I honestly didn't think I could write that many words in a month – especially resembling anything that others would want to read.

I signed up – and participated – because for years I wanted to write a novel. But no matter how much I desired this – no matter how long I waited – I just couldn't get going on it.

I honestly thought if I participated with others in NaNoWriMo during the month of November, I might finally get started... begin a habit of writing... that I could continue after November.

That's all I wanted to do.

—————————— nanowrimo ——————————

Imagine my surprise when my story began changing, new characters showed up, and even more shocking, it went from a child-like, simple Amish story about a young girl who was clumsy – to a suspenseful, romantic tale of unrequited love – and danger for at least one young girl.

That's when I began to feel like an "author".

...and that's when life became more interesting... fun... and scary!

—————————— nanowrimo ——————————

Let every thing that hath breath praise the Lord. Praise ye the Lord.

~ Psalm 150:6

CHAPTER 10

Winning

For those of you who completed the 30 –day challenge – and wrote at least 50,000 words… Congratulations! YOU DID IT!

Be sure you take time to verify your words on the NaNoWriMo website. For the winners, the NaNoWriMo folks have video-taped a little congrats message.

They also have merchandise you can purchase – and access to digital art proclaiming you as a NaNoWriMo WINNER! Pretty cool, huh?

Plus… their sponsors offer some pretty generous gifts to the winners, including huge discounts on software.

... but honestly, you don't have to write 50,000 words to be a winner!

Yes, people who reach the 50,000 –word mark are excited – and they deserve to feel so. They've worked hard and deserve to feel good about what they've achieved. I know I felt great when I finally passed 50,000 words.

Of course, the story usually doesn't stop at 50,000 words. In 2013, I wrote 310 more words to finish my story. And in 2014, well... I wrote over 60,000 words. I don't think I could have done that the first year, but I learned that the story in 2014 was much easier to write, since it wasn't my first time.

But if you did your best, whatever your total word count, I would consider you a WINNER.

I can do all things through Christ which strengtheneth me.

~ Philippians 4:13

CHAPTER 11

Almost; Not Quite

Now let's talk about those who tried, but for whatever reason, couldn't finish out the entire 30 days... or couldn't get to the 50,000 –word goal... or both.

For those of you who completed the 30 –day challenge – and wrote less than 50,000 words... Congratulations! You still accomplished a lot, even if you didn't reach 50,000 words.

Did you give it your best? Did you write on your novel? Then you have every reason to be proud of what you did accomplish. Not everyone can finish... but everyone – at least most who want to try – can begin.

And if you were forced to quit early because of another commitment, keep writing. You don't have to stop on November 30th.

Don't stop until you finish your first draft of your novel. Then let it sit a few weeks – and pick it up, read it, and begin the next step... editing.

If you don't give up, some day you could be looking at a book cover with your name on the front... and who knows – you could become a bestselling author one day!

So keep at it. Never give up.

———— nanowrimo ————

Ye are of God, little children, and have overcome them: because greater is he that is in you, than he that is in the world.

~ 1 John 4:4

CHAPTER 12

What's Next?

I have participated in two NaNoWriMo sessions — November 2013 and November 2014… and I won both times!

I have four novels/ novellas in the works. I also have one novel almost finished. It's steady at around 50,000 words and I'm in the midst of editing it. I have an agent who is interested in seeing it, once I spend enough major hours editing, polishing, and getting it ready for the big showdown.

Okay, I know you're asking… if you have an agent who wants to see it, WHY AREN'T YOU FINISHING IT?

Well, because I entered a contest and sent the **one-sheet** for it… and it didn't even get past the first phase, so now I'm asking myself if it's really any good or not.

The fact that several people have read it – and loved it – hasn't given me enough nerve to actually finish it and send it out for a road test.

For several years, I've been a critique partner (of sorts) for a gentleman who's been writing his memoirs. I say "of sorts" because he has requested my help, but I haven't shared a novel with him to critique. And although I read through his work, watching for continuity and content, I honestly don't know how much of my advice he takes. But he seems to appreciate it, so I feel that I'm being helpful, and it has helped to serve as a learning experience for me.

Another thing to consider is that there is less advice offered on non-fiction writing, and memoirs/ autobiographies. After all, the person is writing about their life experiences.

An editor or critique partner can make suggestions if there are big holes, as well as formatting options (here is where the editing comes in), but otherwise it's more of a challenge to "say less" rather than "more".

I'm also a critique partner and editor for my daughter and for a friend who's written several novels; my friend's agent told her that the grammar and punctuation in her novels was "flawless"... so she asks me to edit all of her work... and she told her friends, who want me to edit their work, too.

So guess who's now taking some classes to be a freelance editor? You guessed it – me. They're harder than I expected; I never knew there was so much to learn about writing fiction novels.

How do I find time to write and edit my own work, plus read and review an average of 15 to 20 books per month, plus write and maintain three blogs – most every day.

I wish I knew... most of the time I stay behind. On a long weekend, sometimes I can catch up, but before I know it, I'm behind again.

———————— *nanowrimo* ————————

Social media!

I found that it's the time I spent on social media that was gobbling up hours of my time each day! The good news is... it CAN be done, too.

So, I had two choices — to either let social media take over my life (which it pretty much did most of the time) or get a chair and a whip and tame that wild animal!

I decided to take the last approach... I began to diligently spend 30 minutes on social media in the mornings, 30 minutes at lunchtime, and 30 minutes after supper. Of course that won't be enough some days, but so far it's been working out great!

... unless I'm posting a review, which shouldn't count

... or chatting with a friend (using Facebook or Google)

... or

Let's face it. I love my social media. I love my online friends! My followers!

YOU RULE, GUYS!

Hey, I'll get the books done. Someday.

I promise.

For the Lord giveth wisdom: out of his mouth cometh knowledge and understanding.

~ Proverbs 2:6

DISCUSSION QUESTIONS

1. NaNoWriMo begins counting the days on November 1, but it starts days, weeks, even months before... read the preparation chapters to discuss the best way to prepare for November 1st.

2. Spend some time brainstorming and generating ideas. Write them down in a notebook. How much do you want to prepare before time to begin?

3. Choose a genre. Fiction or non-fiction? Christian or secular? Mystery? Suspense? Young Adult? Speculative? Romance? Sci-Fi? Historical?

4. A novel outline is a plan for writing a novel. Discuss the different ways of writing... are you a plotter, a pantser, or a combination of both?

5. Who will be your main character(s)? More than one main character can make your novel more complicated to write, but perhaps more interesting.

6. DJ writes about two years of participating in NaNoWriMo. Discuss the differences and the similarities in the two years. Why was it easier to compete the second year?

7. Why did DJ continue to write after she reached 50,000 words?

ACKNOWLEDGEMENTS

First, I want to thank my family and friends for encouraging me to write… and my daughter, for ~~shoving~~ pushing me into participating in the November 2013 NaNoWriMo event.

Next, I want to thank everyone associated with NaNoWriMo, for conceiving such a great idea, as well as all the wonderful people who became online buddies in November 2013-2014.

A special thank you to Suzanne, Jennifer, Ruth, Dana, Rachel, Holly and JC for believing in my work enough to endorse my book.

A very special THANK YOU to my wonderful friend Pam, who sent me to my first writer's workshop – and has always believed in me!

Finally, to my own prayer warriors… Rachel, Sam and Gwen.

nanowrimo

The fear of the Lord is the beginning of knowledge…

~ Proverbs 1:7a

ABOUT THE AUTHOR

DJ Mynatt is a newly-published author who earned a bachelor's degree in networking and a master's degree in Security Management, before beginning a career as an author, editor and speaker. She has also worked full-time for the State of Tennessee for more than 13 years. She lives with her daughter and grandchildren in the beautiful hills of Tennessee.

DJ first began writing in 1990. After her marriage ended, a friend told her it might help to get it all down on paper. So she began… but the words were too sad and she had children to care for, so she set it aside and got a job. She never attempted to write again until her daughter and several friends challenged her to participate in NaNoWriMo… and the rest, as they say, is history!

A member of the American Christian Fiction Writers (ACFW), the Non-Fiction Authors Association (NFAA) and The Christian PEN (TCP), DJ accepts a select few speaking engagements – to make time for writing, editing, blogging, reviewing and attending workshops and writers conferences as time permits.

Be sure to visit DJ online!
djmynatt.com

Do Your Part...

• If you have a personal blog, please consider featuring DJ and her debut novel – *You CAN Write 50,000 Words in 30 Days*

• If you enjoyed reading about DJ's adventures with NaNoWriMo, please consider rating this book and leaving a review on Amazon or GoodReads... it only takes a sentence or two – of course, if you love it and you're inclined to write more, feel free – and THANK YOU!

———————— nanowrimo ————————

Set your affection on things above, not on things on the earth.

~ COLOSSIANS 3:2

ABOUT THE PUBLISHER

CHRISTIAN PUBLISHING FOR HIS GLORY

S&G Publishing offers books with messages that honor
Jesus Christ to the world! S&G works with Christian
authors to bring you the best in "inspirational" fiction
and non-fiction.

S&G is proud to publish a variety of fiction genres:
inspirational romance
young reader
young adult
speculative
historical
suspense

Check out our website at

sgpublish.com

S&G JUNIOR AUTHOR SERIES...
COMING SOON

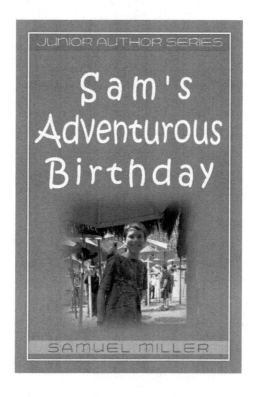

Sam's Birthday Adventure will be available for purchase in JULY!

Samuel is a precocious young man who enjoys drawing, playing with animals of all kinds, and reading.

He also enjoys writing speculative fiction and comics but enjoys telling stories about the road trips he takes with his family as well.

S&G JUNIOR AUTHOR SERIES...
COMING SOON

My Dolphin Friends will be available for purchase in AUGUST!

Gwendolyn is a sweet young lady who – like the stars of **"Dolphin Tale"** *(one of her favorite movies)* – is home-schooled.

She has a deep love of animals. Her dearest wish is to swim with Winter and Hope one day.

S&G CHRISTIAN FICTION...
COMING SOON

ORDER OF THE MOONSTONE SERIES...

BOOK #1 – A RELUCTANT ASSASSIN

RELEASE DATE: SEPTEMBER 29, 2015

S&G COURTSHIP SERIES
TWO VERSIONS AVAILABLE

A **PINK** version

...for HER

S&G COURTSHIP SERIES
TWO VERSIONS AVAILABLE

And a SPECIAL **BLUE** version

...for HIM

Made in the USA
Middletown, DE
06 July 2015